MW01053859

HOW TO GET UNSTUCK FROM THE NEGATIVE MUCK

JOURNAL

HOW TO GET UNSTUCK FROM THE NEGATIVE MUCK JOURNAL

LAKE SULLIVAN, PH.D.

COPYRIGHT © 2013 LAKE SULLIVAN PHD

ISBN-13: 978-0-9853609-3-1

ALL RIGHTS RESERVED. NO PART OF THIS BOOK MAY BE REPRODUCED OR TRANSMITTED IN ANY FORM OR BY ANY MEANS, ELECTRONIC OR MECHANICAL, INCLUDING PHOTOCOPYING, RECORDING, OR BY ANY INFORMATION STORAGE AND RETRIEVAL SYSTEM WITHOUT THE WRITTEN PERMISSION OF THE AUTHOR, EXCEPT WHERE PERMITTED BY LAW.

COVER ILLUSTRATION COPYRIGHT © L SULLIVAN

INTERIOR ILLUSTRATIONS COPYRIGHT © L SULLIVAN

EDITING BY JENNY BOWMAN WWW.JENNYBOWMAN.COM

CONTENTS

HOW TO USE THIS JOURNAL

This journal was made so that you can do the exercises in *How To Get Unstuck From The Negative Muck*. Whenever you see **JOURNAL EXERCISE** in the book get out this journal and do the activity in it.

Have fun learning new ways to say goodbye to bad feelings!

CHAPTER 1

JOURNAL EXERCISES: WHAT IS NEGATIVE MUCK?

JOURNAL EXERCISE: IDENTIFYING THOUGHTS

STEP 1: Set a timer for 2 minutes.

STEP 2: Write down EVERYTHING you think about during those 2 minutes. Even if you think, "I'm not thinking about anything." Write that down too. Write down your thoughts as they come to you in your head. Just as you see or hear them.

_____

_____

_____

_____

_____

_____

_____

_____

_____

_____

_____

_____

_____

_____

_____

_____

_____

_____

STEP 3: Look at all of the things you wrote down and answer the next questions:

1. Are you surprised by anything you wrote down? Why or why not?

_____

_____

_____

_____

_____

_____

_____

2. Did you have any negative thoughts? Write them in the space below. Hint: Negative thoughts can make us feel sad or angry.

_____

_____

_____

_____

_____

_____

_____

3. Did you have any positive thoughts? Write them in the space below. Hint: Positive thoughts are things that we say to ourselves that make us feel happy and excited.

_____

_____

_____

_____

_____

_____

_____

4. Did you have any neutral thoughts? Write them in the space below. Hint: Neutral thoughts aren't positive or negative. You will probably not feel good or bad – you will just have the thought.

_____

_____

_____

_____

_____

_____

_____

JOURNAL EXERCISE: DO YOU GET STUCK IN THE NEGATIVE MUCK?

If you were stuck in the negative muck:

What kind of things would you say to yourself?

_____

_____

_____

_____

_____

_____

_____

_____

If you were stuck in the negative muck, how would you feel?

_____

_____

_____

_____

_____

_____

_____

_____

7

If you were stuck in the negative muck, what would your face look like [draw it here]?

If you were stuck in the negative muck, how would you stand [draw it here]?

If you were stuck in the negative muck, what kind of things would you want to do?

_____

_____

_____

_____

_____

_____

_____

_____

What kind of things would you NOT want to do?

_____

_____

_____

_____

_____

_____

_____

_____

_____

Can you name a time when you felt sad about something that happened in your life? What happened?

_____

_____

_____

_____

_____

_____

_____

_____

_____

_____

_____

_____

_____

_____

_____

_____

_____

_____

_____

Can you draw a picture of what you looked like when this sad event happened? Make sure to draw your face and the way you were standing or sitting. Put some thought bubbles above your head and write in some of the things you said to yourself. Draw it here.

How did you act when you were feeling sad?

_____

_____

_____

_____

_____

_____

_____

Did you do anything that made you feel worse? For example, did you not talk to others about what was bothering you? Did you stay in your room all day?

_____

_____

_____

_____

_____

_____

_____

What did you do to make yourself feel better?

_____

_____

_____

_____

_____

CHAPTER 2

JOURNAL EXERCISES: HOW TO SOLVE PROBLEMS YOU CAN CHANGE

STEPS TO SOLVING A PROBLEM

There are five steps to solving problems (see the problem solving chart below):

STEP #1: Write down the problem.

STEP #2: Write down all the ways you could solve the problem (these are called "solutions"). It doesn't matter if some of the ideas are wacky or not likely to happen, write them down anyway. Make sure to also write down ways to solve the problem that would be easy to try.

STEP #3: Go through each of your solutions and write down what will probably happen if you go through with it.

STEP #4: Pick a solution that you think will work best. Ask an adult to help you with this step.

STEP #5: Follow through with the solution. Then come back and write down how well it worked. Give the solution a grade. Give it an "A" if it worked perfectly. Give it a "B" if it worked, but was not a perfect solution. Give it a "C" if it was just okay. Give it a "D" if it didn't work very well, but you

JOURNAL EXERCISE: HOW TO SOLVE A PROBLEM

Use the problem solving charts below and try to solve these problems:

Pretend that you can't find your favorite hat in your closet. Go through all five of the problem-solving steps to figure out a solution. Fill in the chart below.

HOW TO SOLVE A PROBLEM:

WHAT IS THE PROBLEM THAT I'M HAVING?	SOLUTION #1:	WHAT WOULD PROBABLY HAPPEN IF I USED SOLUTION #1?	IS #1 THE BEST SOLUTION? WHY OR WHY NOT?	IF YOU CHOSE SOLUTION #1, DID IT WORK? (GIVE IT A GRADE OF A, B, C, D, OR F)
	SOLUTION #2:	WHAT WOULD PROBABLY HAPPEN IF I USED SOLUTION #2?	IS #2 THE BEST SOLUTION? WHY OR WHY NOT?	IF YOU CHOSE SOLUTION #2, DID IT WORK? (GIVE IT A GRADE OF A, B, C, D, OR F)
	SOLUTION #3:	WHAT WOULD PROBABLY HAPPEN IF I USED SOLUTION #3?	IS #3 THE BEST SOLUTION? WHY OR WHY NOT?	IF YOU CHOSE SOLUTION #3, DID IT WORK? (GIVE IT A GRADE OF A, B, C, D, OR F)

Pretend that you lost your backpack at school.
Go through all five of the problem-solving
steps to figure out a solution.

HOW TO SOLVE A PROBLEM:

WHAT IS THE PROBLEM THAT I'M HAVING?				
SOLUTION #1:	WHAT WOULD PROBABLY HAPPEN IF I USED SOLUTION #1?	IS #1 THE BEST SOLUTION? WHY OR WHY NOT?	IF YOU CHOSE SOLUTION #1, DID IT WORK? (GIVE IT A GRADE OF A, B, C, D, OR F)	
SOLUTION #2:	WHAT WOULD PROBABLY HAPPEN IF I USED SOLUTION #2?	IS #2 THE BEST SOLUTION? WHY OR WHY NOT?	IF YOU CHOSE SOLUTION #2, DID IT WORK? (GIVE IT A GRADE OF A, B, C, D, OR F)	
SOLUTION #3:	WHAT WOULD PROBABLY HAPPEN IF I USED SOLUTION #3?	IS #3 THE BEST SOLUTION? WHY OR WHY NOT?	IF YOU CHOSE SOLUTION #3, DID IT WORK? (GIVE IT A GRADE OF A, B, C, D, OR F)	

Pretend that you are walking your dog. All of a sudden a car drives by fast and it scares your dog so much that the dog pulls you until you drop the leash. Your dog runs away. Go through all five of the problem-solving steps to figure out what to do.

HOW TO SOLVE A PROBLEM:

WHAT IS THE PROBLEM THAT I'M HAVING?		WHAT WOULD PROBABLY HAPPEN IF I USED SOLUTION #1?	IS #1 THE BEST SOLUTION? WHY OR WHY NOT?	IF YOU CHOSE SOLUTION #1, DID IT WORK? (GIVE IT A GRADE OF A, B, C, D, OR F)
	SOLUTION #1:			
	SOLUTION #2:	WHAT WOULD PROBABLY HAPPEN IF I USED SOLUTION #2?	IS #2 THE BEST SOLUTION? WHY OR WHY NOT?	IF YOU CHOSE SOLUTION #2, DID IT WORK? (GIVE IT A GRADE OF A, B, C, D, OR F)
	SOLUTION #3:	WHAT WOULD PROBABLY HAPPEN IF I USED SOLUTION #3?	IS #3 THE BEST SOLUTION? WHY OR WHY NOT?	IF YOU CHOSE SOLUTION #3, DID IT WORK? (GIVE IT A GRADE OF A, B, C, D, OR F)

Pretend that you have two friends at school. One day they both decide they do not want to play with you. Go through all five of the problem-solving steps to figure out what to do.

HOW TO SOLVE A PROBLEM:

WHAT IS THE PROBLEM THAT I'M HAVING?				
	SOLUTION #1:	WHAT WOULD PROBABLY HAPPEN IF I USED SOLUTION #1?	IS #1 THE BEST SOLUTION? WHY OR WHY NOT?	IF YOU CHOSE SOLUTION #1, DID IT WORK? (GIVE IT A GRADE OF A, B, C, D, OR F)
	SOLUTION #2:	WHAT WOULD PROBABLY HAPPEN IF I USED SOLUTION #2?	IS #2 THE BEST SOLUTION? WHY OR WHY NOT?	IF YOU CHOSE SOLUTION #2, DID IT WORK? (GIVE IT A GRADE OF A, B, C, D, OR F)
	SOLUTION #3:	WHAT WOULD PROBABLY HAPPEN IF I USED SOLUTION #3?	IS #3 THE BEST SOLUTION? WHY OR WHY NOT?	IF YOU CHOSE SOLUTION #3, DID IT WORK? (GIVE IT A GRADE OF A, B, C, D, OR F)

Now come up with a problem that you are facing. Go through all five of the problem-solving steps to figure out what to do.

HOW TO SOLVE A PROBLEM:

WHAT IS THE PROBLEM THAT I'M HAVING?		WHAT WOULD PROBABLY HAPPEN IF I USED SOLUTION #1?	IS #1 THE BEST SOLUTION? WHY OR WHY NOT?	IF YOU CHOSE SOLUTION #1, DID IT WORK? (GIVE IT A GRADE OF A, B, C, D, OR F)
	SOLUTION #1:			
	SOLUTION #2:	WHAT WOULD PROBABLY HAPPEN IF I USED SOLUTION #2?	IS #2 THE BEST SOLUTION? WHY OR WHY NOT?	IF YOU CHOSE SOLUTION #2, DID IT WORK? (GIVE IT A GRADE OF A, B, C, D, OR F)
	SOLUTION #3:	WHAT WOULD PROBABLY HAPPEN IF I USED SOLUTION #3?	IS #3 THE BEST SOLUTION? WHY OR WHY NOT?	IF YOU CHOSE SOLUTION #3, DID IT WORK? (GIVE IT A GRADE OF A, B, C, D, OR F)

CHAPTER 3

JOURNAL EXERCISES: HOW TO COPE WITH PROBLEMS YOU CAN'T CHANGE

JOURNAL EXERCISE: HOW DO YOU COPE?

Think of a problem you are having and write down 3 healthy ways that you can cope with that problem.

_____

_____

_____

_____

_____

_____

_____

_____

_____

_____

_____

_____

_____

_____

_____

_____

_____

_____

CHAPTER 4

JOURNAL EXERCISES: UNDERSTANDING SELF-TALK

JOURNAL EXERCISE: SELF-TALK

Here are four situations that kids often go through. Can you write down what the kids may be saying to themselves?

SITUATION #1:

Paige is playing with her dog, Prince, outside. They are playing with a Frisbee and Prince is excitedly running around trying to catch it in the air. It's a bright and sunny day.

What are some things that Paige may be saying to herself (self-talk)?

_____

_____

_____

_____

SITUATION #2:

Jaden is brushing his teeth.

What are some things that he may be saying to himself (self-talk)?

_____

_____

_____

_____

_____

_____

_____

SITUATION #3:

Samantha goes outside for recess. She sees that her three best friends are using the only jump rope available. They look happy and are stopping every once in awhile to whisper things to each other.

What are some things that Samantha may be saying to herself (self-talk)?

_____

_____

_____

_____

_____

_____

SITUATION #4:

Timothy got back his grade for a science project that he worked really hard on. The grade was much lower than he expected.

What are some things that Timothy may be saying to himself?

_____

_____

_____

_____

_____

_____

_____

_____

CHAPTER 5

JOURNAL EXERCISES: CREATING OPPOSITES FOR NEGATIVE SELF-TALK MESSAGES

EXERCISE: POSITIVE STATEMENTS ALL AROUND

Choose 3 positive statements from the lists given in the book. Choose ones that you think would help you be more positive in your life. Write those statements in big, bold letters on the 3 pages that follow. Decorate those three pages with positive drawings of whatever you choose. Cut the 3 pages out of your journal. Hang the three statements in your room where you can see them everyday.

JOURNAL EXERCISES: THE FOUR FLAVORS OF NEGATIVE SELF-TALK MESSAGES & HOW TO TALK BACK TO THEM

JOURNAL EXERCISE: ALL OR NOTHING THINKING IN OTHERS

Michael likes to hang out with his older brother Robert. Sometimes Robert lets him come along when he meets up with his friends to ride bikes. But, lately Robert has not wanted Michael around him. And today, Robert flat out says, "No!" when Michael asks to go with him.

If Michael was having All or Nothing thinking, what are some things he would say to himself? (Hint: Make sure to use words like: "always," "everything," "never," or "nothing.") Ask an adult if you get stuck.

_____

_____

_____

_____

_____

_____

_____

_____

_____

_____

Now, what could he say (self-talk) that DOES NOT use All or Nothing thinking? (Hint: Try to take out words like, "always, " "everything," "never," or "nothing." Instead, use words like, "this time," "sometimes," or "some things.")

_____

_____

_____

_____

_____

_____

_____

_____

_____

_____

JOURNAL EXERCISE: YOUR ALL OR NOTHING THINKING

Keep your journal with you for one day. Pay attention to any time you think or say the words, "always," "everything," "never," or "nothing." You can be in any situation when you think or say these words. Write down what you were thinking or what you said out loud.

_____

_____

_____

_____

_____

_____

_____

_____

_____

_____

_____

_____

_____

_____

_____

_____

_____

_____

_____

_____

_____

_____

_____

_____

_____

_____

_____

_____

_____

_____

_____

_____

_____

_____

_____

_____

Next, write down things you can say to yourself instead without using the words, "always," "everything," "never," or "nothing." (Hint: Try to use words like, "this time," "sometimes," or "some things.")

_____

_____

_____

_____

_____

_____

_____

_____

_____

_____

_____

_____

_____

_____

_____

_____

_____

_____

_____

JOURNAL EXERCISE: FORTUNE-TELLING

Keep your journal with you for another day. Pay attention to any time you think you know the ending to a situation that is happening to you. You can be in any situation when you have these thoughts.. Write down what you think will happen to you. Try to give as many details as you can think of.

_____

_____

_____

_____

_____

_____

_____

_____

_____

_____

_____

_____

_____

_____

_____

_____

_____

_____

_____

_____

_____

_____

_____

_____

_____

_____

_____

_____

_____

_____

_____

_____

_____

_____

Next, write down what actually happened in real life. Notice any differences between what you thought would happen and what actually happened. Take special notice of any fortune-telling thoughts that you had that were negative. Did things end up as bad as you thought they would be? Why or why not?

_____

_____

_____

_____

_____

_____

_____

_____

_____

_____

_____

_____

_____

_____

_____

_____

_____

_____

_____

_____

_____

_____

_____

_____

_____

_____

_____

_____

_____

_____

_____

_____

_____

_____

_____

If the situation ended up as bad as you thought it would be, how did you cope? Could you have used any other healthy coping skills you learned about earlier in the book?

_____

_____

_____

_____

_____

_____

_____

_____

If things didn't turn out as bad as you thought they would, what could you have said to yourself to stop the negative fortune-telling?

_____

_____

_____

_____

_____

_____

JOURNAL EXERCISE: MIND-READING

Keep your journal with you for another day. Pay attention to any time you think you know what another person is thinking about you. You can be in any situation when you have these thoughts.. Write down what you think they were thinking about you.

_____

_____

_____

_____

_____

_____

_____

_____

_____

_____

_____

_____

_____

_____

_____

_____

_____

Next, write down other thoughts that they could have been thinking like in the example above. Remember, most people think about a lot of things. So, be sure to write down things that aren't about you at all!

_____

_____

_____

_____

_____

_____

_____

_____

_____

_____

_____

_____

_____

_____

_____

JOURNAL EXERCISE: "SHOULD" STATEMENTS

Keep your journal with you for another day. Pay attention to any time you think or say that you "should" do something. You can be in any situation when you have these thoughts. Write down what you said to yourself. Write down how you felt after you said the "should" statement.

_____

_____

_____

_____

_____

_____

_____

_____

_____

_____

_____

_____

_____

_____

_____

_____

_____

Next, write down other things you can say to yourself without using the "should" word. Hint: Try rewriting your "should" statement using the words, "It would be great if..." or "I wish I could..."

_____

_____

_____

_____

_____

_____

_____

_____

Write down how you feel after reading your rewritten statement. Does this new statement make you feel different than the "should" statement? If you feel different reading the new statement, why do you think this happened? Do you think that you felt different because the new statement puts less pressure on you?

_____

_____

_____

_____

_____
_____
_____
_____
_____
_____
_____
_____
_____
_____
_____
_____
_____
_____
_____
_____
_____
_____
_____
_____

JOURNAL EXERCISE: MAGNIFICATION

Keep your journal with you for another day. Pay attention to any time you begin to focus too much on bad things. Write down what a news announcer would say about the bad things if Bad News Radio was talking to you.

_____

_____

_____

_____

_____

_____

_____

_____

_____

_____

_____

Next, write down other good things that are going on in your life that you can focus on instead. Write down what a news announcer would say if the program changed to Good News Radio.

_____

_____

_____

_____

_____

_____

_____

_____

_____

CHAPTER 7

JOURNAL EXERCISES: HOW TO KEEP FROM GETTING STUCK IN THE NEGATIVE MUCK!

JOURNAL EXERCISE: HOW DO I FEEL?

You've already learned how to pay close attention to your thoughts in the book. So, now all you have to do is practice, practice, practice! This journal exercise will help you learn how to pay attention to your feelings.

HOW TO PAY ATTENTION TO YOUR FEELINGS

Paying attention to your feelings is not very hard to learn. First, take a look at this list of feelings:

HAPPY
CONTENT
NEUTRAL
CONFUSED
SAD
SCARED
ANGRY
DISCOURAGED

Then, every day for the next two weeks, find a time to write in this journal. See the chart below to see how your journal entry can appear. Figure out how you are feeling based on the list and then write down your feelings in your diary. If you have feelings other than the ones on the list, feel free to write those down instead.

Once you write down your feelings, try to figure out some thoughts that you are having that are making you feel better or worse about what is going on in your life. If you get stuck and need help, ask an adult to help you.

If you are having positive thoughts - excellent! If you are having negative thoughts - no problem. Just go back to the things you learned earlier in the book about talking back to negative self-talk messages and write down ways you can talk back to those negative thoughts.

HOW TO PAY ATTENTION TO YOUR FEELINGS:

DATE:	FEELING?	THOUGHTS THAT ARE MAKING ME FEEL BETTER?	THOUGHTS THAT ARE MAKING ME FEEL WORSE?	THINGS I CAN SAY TO MYSELF TO TALK BACK TO NEGATIVE THOUGHTS:
	HAPPY CONTENT NEUTRAL CONFUSED SAD SCARED ANGRY DISCOURAGED OTHER:			
	HAPPY CONTENT NEUTRAL CONFUSED SAD SCARED ANGRY DISCOURAGED OTHER:			
	HAPPY CONTENT NEUTRAL CONFUSED SAD SCARED ANGRY DISCOURAGED OTHER:			

HOW TO PAY ATTENTION TO YOUR FEELINGS:

DATE:	FEELING? HAPPY CONFUSED ANGRY OTHER: CONTENT SAD DISCOURAGED NEUTRAL SCARED	THOUGHTS THAT ARE MAKING ME FEEL BETTER?	THOUGHTS THAT ARE MAKING ME FEEL WORSE?	THINGS I CAN SAY TO MYSELF TO TALK BACK TO NEGATIVE THOUGHTS:
DATE:	FEELING? HAPPY CONFUSED ANGRY OTHER: CONTENT SAD DISCOURAGED NEUTRAL SCARED	THOUGHTS THAT ARE MAKING ME FEEL BETTER?	THOUGHTS THAT ARE MAKING ME FEEL WORSE?	THINGS I CAN SAY TO MYSELF TO TALK BACK TO NEGATIVE THOUGHTS:
DATE:	FEELING? HAPPY CONFUSED ANGRY OTHER: CONTENT SAD DISCOURAGED NEUTRAL SCARED	THOUGHTS THAT ARE MAKING ME FEEL BETTER?	THOUGHTS THAT ARE MAKING ME FEEL WORSE?	THINGS I CAN SAY TO MYSELF TO TALK BACK TO NEGATIVE THOUGHTS:

HOW TO PAY ATTENTION TO YOUR FEELINGS:

DATE:	FEELING?	THOUGHTS THAT ARE MAKING ME FEEL BETTER?	THOUGHTS THAT ARE MAKING ME FEEL WORSE?	THINGS I CAN SAY TO MYSELF TO TALK BACK TO NEGATIVE THOUGHTS:
	HAPPY CONFUSED ANGRY OTHER: CONTENT SAD DISCOURAGED NEUTRAL SCARED			
DATE:	FEELING? HAPPY CONFUSED ANGRY OTHER: CONTENT SAD DISCOURAGED NEUTRAL SCARED	THOUGHTS THAT ARE MAKING ME FEEL BETTER?	THOUGHTS THAT ARE MAKING ME FEEL WORSE?	THINGS I CAN SAY TO MYSELF TO TALK BACK TO NEGATIVE THOUGHTS:
DATE:	FEELING? HAPPY CONFUSED ANGRY OTHER: CONTENT SAD DISCOURAGED NEUTRAL SCARED	THOUGHTS THAT ARE MAKING ME FEEL BETTER?	THOUGHTS THAT ARE MAKING ME FEEL WORSE?	THINGS I CAN SAY TO MYSELF TO TALK BACK TO NEGATIVE THOUGHTS:

HOW TO PAY ATTENTION TO YOUR FEELINGS:

DATE:	FEELING? HAPPY CONTENT NEUTRAL CONFUSED SAD SCARED ANGRY DISCOURAGED OTHER:	THOUGHTS THAT ARE MAKING ME FEEL BETTER?	THOUGHTS THAT ARE MAKING ME FEEL WORSE?	THINGS I CAN SAY TO MYSELF TO TALK BACK TO NEGATIVE THOUGHTS:
DATE:	FEELING? HAPPY CONTENT NEUTRAL CONFUSED SAD SCARED ANGRY DISCOURAGED OTHER:	THOUGHTS THAT ARE MAKING ME FEEL BETTER?	THOUGHTS THAT ARE MAKING ME FEEL WORSE?	THINGS I CAN SAY TO MYSELF TO TALK BACK TO NEGATIVE THOUGHTS:
DATE:	FEELING? HAPPY CONTENT NEUTRAL CONFUSED SAD SCARED ANGRY DISCOURAGED OTHER:	THOUGHTS THAT ARE MAKING ME FEEL BETTER?	THOUGHTS THAT ARE MAKING ME FEEL WORSE?	THINGS I CAN SAY TO MYSELF TO TALK BACK TO NEGATIVE THOUGHTS:

HOW TO PAY ATTENTION TO YOUR FEELINGS:

DATE:	FEELING? HAPPY CONTENT NEUTRAL CONFUSED SAD SCARED ANGRY DISCOURAGED OTHER:	THOUGHTS THAT ARE MAKING ME FEEL BETTER?	THOUGHTS THAT ARE MAKING ME FEEL WORSE?	THINGS I CAN SAY TO MYSELF TO TALK BACK TO NEGATIVE THOUGHTS:
DATE:	FEELING? HAPPY CONTENT NEUTRAL CONFUSED SAD SCARED ANGRY DISCOURAGED OTHER:	THOUGHTS THAT ARE MAKING ME FEEL BETTER?	THOUGHTS THAT ARE MAKING ME FEEL WORSE?	THINGS I CAN SAY TO MYSELF TO TALK BACK TO NEGATIVE THOUGHTS:
DATE:	FEELING? HAPPY CONTENT NEUTRAL CONFUSED SAD SCARED ANGRY DISCOURAGED OTHER:	THOUGHTS THAT ARE MAKING ME FEEL BETTER?	THOUGHTS THAT ARE MAKING ME FEEL WORSE?	THINGS I CAN SAY TO MYSELF TO TALK BACK TO NEGATIVE THOUGHTS:

Made in the USA
Las Vegas, NV
12 December 2024

13934834R00044